KIDS' DAY OUT

Amusement Parks and Water Parks

Joanne Mattern

Peachtree

RED CHAIR ·PRESS·

Kids' Day Out is produced and published by Red Chair Press:

Red Chair Press LLC   PO Box 333   South Egremont, MA 01258-0333

www.redchairpress.com

Publisher's Cataloging-In-Publication Data

Names: Mattern, Joanne, 1963–

Title: Amusement parks and water parks / Joanne Mattern.

Description: Egremont, MA : Red Chair Press, [2018] | Series: Kids' day out | Interest age level: 007-010. | Includes index, glossary and resources for more information. | Summary: "Today's amusement parks are filled with amazing, high-tech rides. Some even take the fun to the water! Amusement parks of the past were exciting places as well. Amusement parks have been around for hundreds of years. Readers discover the history of these fun-filled places!"-- Provided by publisher.

Identifiers: ISBN 978-1-63440-388-7 (library hardcover) | ISBN 978-1-63440-392-4 (ebook)

Subjects: LCSH: Amusement parks--History--Juvenile literature. | CYAC: Amusement parks-- History.

Classification: LCC GV1851.A35 M38 2018 (print) | LCC GV1851.A35 DDC 791.068--dc23

Photo credits: Cover, p. 1, 3, 4, 5, 6, 7, 24, 25, 27, 28, 29, 30: iStock; p. 10, 12, 13, 18, 23: Alamy; p. 11, 14, 15, 16, 17: Library of Congress; p. 8, 9, 26: Dreamstime; p. 19, 20, 21: Getty Images

Printed in the United States of America

0518 1P CGBF18

Contents

A Place for Fun!

Have you ever been to an amusement park? Amusement parks can be a lot of fun. These parks include many different kinds of rides, from roller coasters to Ferris wheels. There are usually places to eat and games to play at amusement parks as well.

Some amusement parks take the fun to the water! Water parks can have swimming pools and giant slides. There are lots of ways to have fun at these parks.

Today's amusement parks are filled with amazing, high-tech rides. However, amusement parks of the past were exciting places as well. Amusement parks have been around for hundreds of years. Let's explore these fun-filled places!

Fairs and Fun

musement parks got their start about 500 years ago. In those days, many towns held fairs. Fairs were usually held once a year on a holiday or religious feast day. A fair usually had lots of people selling different things. There were stalls selling food. Performers walked around the fair singing, dancing, and doing tricks. Sometimes there were animal rides and games for children to enjoy.

Between 1550 and 1700, many European cities had pleasure gardens. These gardens were open areas next to inns and taverns. People could relax and enjoy food and drink in these gardens.

In 1583, the world's first amusement park opened in Denmark. It was called Bakken. At first, Bakken only had entertainment and people selling goods and foods. During the 1800s, rides were added.

In 1661, Vauxhall Gardens opened along the Thames River in London. People could walk the garden paths. They could see acrobats and other performers, watch fireworks, and listen to music.

During the late 1800s, people began using steam to make mechanical rides. One of the first was a steam-powered carousel. Mechanical rides began to appear at fairs and in parks. The rides were popular, and soon many more rides appeared.

America had pleasure gardens as well. Just like in Europe, many were near hotels. Others were built at the end of trolley lines. People would ride the trolley and enjoy a fun day outside in the park.

Starting in April, 1893, the city of Chicago held a huge fair called the World's Columbian Exposition. This was the first fair to put all rides and shows in a separate area. This area was called the midway. Thousands of people visited the Exposition. They enjoyed the rides and the other attractions. The Exposition was a huge success.

The fair in Chicago featured people in costumes from around the world and rides never before seen!

One of the highlights of the Exposition was the first Ferris wheel. The wheel was built by George W. Ferris. It was an amazing feat of engineering. No one had ever tried to build anything like it.

The Exposition Ferris wheel stood 140 feet tall. It measured 250 feet across and 825 feet around. A huge 89,320-pound axle turned the ride. The wheel held 36 cars. Each car held 60 people and went around the wheel nine times.

The first Ferris Wheel, 1893 in Chicago

New York City's Coney Island became one of the most famous and popular early amusement parks. This five-mile stretch of beach was near the crowded streets of the city. In 1884, Lamarcus Thompson built a small train ride on Coney Island. The Switchback Railroad had two tracks that ran down a 600-foot-long structure. The ride earned more than $600 a day.

A young man named George Tilyou built a small Ferris wheel at Coney Island in 1894. The Ferris wheel was the most popular attraction at the park for many years.

Tilyou's Ferris wheel was so successful he decided to add more rides. In 1897, he bought a ride called the Steeplechase Horses. Riders raced mechanical horses down a long metal racetrack. Later, Tilyou added other mechanical attractions.

Coney Island was also home to one of the first water parks. In 1895, Captain Paul Boyton opened Sea Lion Park. The park included a water slide called Shoot the Chutes. Boyton also performed swimming demonstrations at the park.

Sea Lion Park closed in 1903. The area was bought by two businessmen. They opened Luna Park on the site in 1930. Luna Park was lit by a million electric lights and had a tall Electric Tower of lights. Electric lights were just becoming popular and people came just to see the lighted park. Visitors paid 10 cents for children's rides and 25 cents for bigger adult rides.

In 1904, another park opened nearby. This park was called Dreamland. Like the other parks on Coney Island, Dreamland featured many different rides, including boats and trains. The park was a popular attraction until 1911. That year, a fire burned the whole park to the ground.

Crazy Coasters

During the late 1800s, new and exciting rides began to appear. One of the most exciting was the roller coaster. No one is sure who built the first roller coaster, but many historians believe these rides began in Russia or France in the early 1800s.

The first roller coaster in America was the Mauch Chunk Switchback Railway in Pennsylvania. These train tracks once carried carts to coal mines. Later, they were made into a runaway-train roller coaster.

It's a Fact

During the 1700s, many people in Russia enjoyed ice slides. Several inches of ice covered a steep wooden frame. People climbed stairs to the top and slid down the ice to the bottom.

In 1928, these kids enjoyed the White City roller coaster in Chicago.

By the 1920s, people were enjoying even more exciting roller coasters, such as White City Amusement Park in Chicago and the Flying Turns in Ohio. Many roller coasters included tunnels that plunged riders into darkness as they raced down the track.

Disney Goes Big

Many amusement parks closed during the 1930s and the 1940s because of the Great Depression and World War II. By the 1950s, people had large families and money to spend. Walt Disney, a man who made popular movies and television shows, decided to open an amusement park.

Disneyland opened in California in July 1955. The park included rides and other attractions based on Disney characters and movies. Families loved the idea. Disneyland soon became the most popular park in the world.

In 1971, Walt Disney World opened in Florida. It is the largest theme park ever built. Other Disney parks were built around the world.

Wild Water

Water rides are also popular attractions at amusement parks. Many parks include a log flume ride. Riders zoom down a steep hill and land in a pool of water at the bottom with a big splash. Other parks include bumper boats or simple boat rides for children. Areas where children can wade or splash in sprays of water are also popular.

The first big water park was Wet 'n' Wild, which opened in Orlando, Florida, in 1977. The park featured a lazy river where people could float along in large inner tubes. Another popular attraction was a wave pool.

Today there are hundreds of water parks around the world. Some are located in warm places and are open all year. Others are open only during the summer. And some water parks are indoors, so people can enjoy wet and wild fun all year long.

The first indoor water park was built in Edmonton, Alberta, Canada in 1985 in the huge Edmonton Mall.

Thrill Rides

As the years passed, amusement park rides became bigger and scarier. Large parks, such as the Six Flags parks around the United States, built new rides every year. These rides included thrilling features such as terrifying drops, cars that traveled upside-down, seats that let a rider's legs hang free, and sharp twists and turns.

Roller coasters aren't the only wild rides at parks. Popular rides include trains that carry riders through the dark and scare them with haunted scenes and special effects. Other rides toss their riders from side to side. Some rides spin in a circle so riders hang upside-down. It seems like people are always looking for new ways to be scared and thrilled at amusement parks!

Staying Safe

Amusement parks are a lot of fun, but they can also create danger. To keep riders and visitors safe, all amusement park rides have safety features. Many rides include seat belts. On some rides, bars lock into place to keep riders in their seats. Other rides have enclosed cars to keep people from falling out.

People who work at amusement parks test the rides many times before parks open. They make sure everything is working properly. If a ride is not working right, it is shut down until someone can fix the problem.

Visitors to parks also must follow rules when they go on rides. Riders should never hang out of cars or stand up and move around while a ride is in motion. Following rules and staying safe make amusement parks more fun for everyone.

The Future of Fun

Just as in the past, today's amusement parks offer thrills and fun for the whole family. Young children can enjoy gentle rides, while older teens and adults can ride on thrilling roller  coasters and other exciting rides. Some people travel from park to park to enjoy rides that are famous all over the world. There is so much to do and see at amusement parks!

Amusement parks began as a way for people to have fun outside and do something different with their time. Today, the dream of excitement and fun lives on in amusement and water parks around the world.

Glossary

attractions things or places that create interest or excitement

axle a rod in the center of a wheel

entertainment something that creates enjoyment

exhibitions public displays

exposition a large public exhibit

mechanical operated by machine

midway an area of a fair where rides and games are located

pavilion an open building that is used for a show or exhibit

steeplechase a kind of horse race

trolley an electric streetcar that runs on tracks

Learn More in the Library

Books

Brown, Jordan D. *The Thrills and Chills of Amusement Parks.* Simon Spotlight, 2015.

Hamilton, S.L. *Water Parks (Wild Water).* Abdo, 2015.

10 Best Theme Parks for Families*
*from *Parents Magazine*, 2014, 2016

Legoland, Carlsbad, California

Disneyland, Anaheim, California

Disney's Magic Kingdom, Orlando, Florida

Universal's Islands of Adventure, Orlando, Florida

Sesame Place, Langhorne, Pennsylvania

Disney's Animal Kingdom, Orlando, Florida

Hersheypark, Hershey, Pennsylvania

Cedar Point, Sandusky, Ohio

Story Land, Glen, New Hampshire

Six Flags Fiesta Park, San Antonio, Texas

Index

About the Author

Joanne Mattern is the author of many nonfiction books for children. She enjoys writing about animals, history, and famous people and loves to bring science and history to life for young readers. Joanne lives in New York State with her husband, four children, and several pets and enjoys reading and music.